T0033345

The
WISDOM
of BIRDS

About the Author

Alison Davies is the author of several fiction and non-fiction books including *Be More Cat*, *Be More Dog* and *Written in the Stars: Constellations, Facts and Folklore*. She writes for a wide selection of magazines and her features have also appeared in *The Times Educational Supplement* and the *Sunday Express*, among others.

About the Illustrator

John James Audubon (1785–1851) was an American ornithologist and naturalist, as well as a self-taught wildlife artist. The 435 prints in his book, *Birds of America*, which was printed between 1827 and 1838, is a collection of his beautifully engraved prints on paper that showcase the vibrant colours and diversity of birds found in North America, and is considered to be the archetype of wildlife illustration.

The
WISDOM
of BIRDS

Essential Life Lessons for
Positivity and Grace

Alison Davies

First published in Great Britain in 2024 by LOM ART, an imprint of
Michael O'Mara Books Limited
9 Lion Yard
Tremadoc Road
London SW4 7NQ

A CIP catalogue record for this book is available from the British Library.

This product is made of material from well-managed, FSC®-certified
forests and other controlled sources. The manufacturing processes
conform to the environmental regulations of the country of origin.

ISBN: 978-1-915751-14-0 in hardback print format
ISBN: 978-1-915751-15-7 in ebook format

1 2 3 4 5 6 7 8 9 10

www.mombooks.com

Designed and typeset by Ana Bjezancevic

Printed and bound in China

MIX
Paper | Supporting
responsible forestry
FSC® C020056
FSC
www.fsc.org

Introduction

Throughout history and across cultures, birds have long
held a very special place in our hearts, and it's easy to
see why. Whether they're commanding the skies with
grace and fortitude or traversing the waters beneath in
a fluid dance that dips, dives and glides to a destination
of their choosing, they have a way of stealing the show.
Some are happier on the ground, foraging and making
a nest beneath the leaves, while other treehoppers take
delight in the dense canopy of branches, from which
they can leap and flit to their heart's content. Then there
are those who crave the thrill of the mountains or feel
most at home beneath a blanket of snow. Whatever
their preferred place to roam, it doesn't matter, for
every bird has a unique gift or skill to be admired.

There are those blessed with a colourful plumage, the intricately patterned, or bright daubed beauties that always make a statement. Then there are clever ones who blend into the landscape, the resourceful collectors, and the ones that flock together finding safety and community in numbers. There are the songbirds with their operatic melodies, the squawkers and the squabblers, and the mimics with a flair for the dramatic which they use to their advantage.

But although they vary throughout the globe, the one thing they have in common is a story and a lesson which they can teach us. It might not seem obvious at first, but as you learn a little about each one, the gift becomes apparent. Here, within the pages of this book, you will find sixty of the world's most enchanting birds laid out with beautiful illustrations by Victorian ornothologist and wildlife artist John James Audubon. You will unearth what makes each one special, and how their lesson can help you in your own life. Take a breath and take flight amid these pages to discover the wisdom of birds.

Be proud of who you are

BELTED KINGFISHER

Named after the Anglo-Saxon word meaning 'king
of fishes', these shaggy-crested birds are usually seen
patrolling waterways and riversides or standing loud and
proud. Native to North America, the belted kingfisher is
a wanderer at heart and has graced the shores of Hawaii,
the Galapagos islands, Greenland, the Netherlands and
even the British Isles. While long commutes might be
unusual for other types of kingfisher, the belted variety
has a bold inquisitive streak, and a need to impress
its presence wherever the fancy takes. With a raucous
cry, this bird says, 'I'm here, I'm ready, this is me!'

Find your space to shine

MANX SHEERWATER

Named after the island it once dominated, the manx sheerwater had its largest colony on the Isle of Man, but thanks to an invasion of rats over 200 years ago this was swiftly destroyed, meaning the bird had to travel further afield to establish itself and truly flourish. Now it nests along the Atlantic coast in deeply crafted burrows but spends most of its time out at sea. While it may appear ungainly on the land, its slender body lends itself to gliding and this bird is able to fly at speed over the surface of the water, 'sheering' a path through the waves.

Let positivity be your light

PROTHONOTARY WARBLER

This colourful charmer is a fan of swampy environments
and likes to migrate south, following the Atlantic over the
Gulf of Mexico. While its surroundings may be seriously
murky, the prothonotary warbler goes its own way, offering
a much-needed glimpse of brightness and a youthful
energy to the vista. Couple this with a habit of nesting in
standing dead trees, and you begin to see a pattern forming.
This sunny songbird brings light to the darkest places and
gets its 'prothonotary' moniker from the golden robes
worn by papal clerks in the Roman Catholic Church.

Find joy in togetherness

AMERICAN GOLDFINCH

A symbol of hope, celebration and rebirth in many
cultures around the world, the American goldfinch is
charm personified, from the vibrant golden feathers
and striking markings of the adult male to the joyful
way it flits from tree to tree. The female's olive hue may
be less colourful, but she is still a beauty and the two
share dominance throughout the seasons. This unity
also appears in their flight calls, which mimic each
other and help other members of the flock distinguish a
pairing. Togetherness is at the heart of this bird's success,
and their message is as harmonious as their song.

Go with the flow

ARCTIC TERN

These clever birds know that to take the arduous journey from the Arctic to the Antarctic Circle they must work with the elements, which means releasing all expectation and allowing the breeze to carry them forwards to their destination. Found along the eastern coast of South America, in Europe, Iceland, Australia, New Zealand and the Pacific Islands, these graceful sea birds are made for migration. Small in build, with narrow wings that allow them to glide in an aerial dance akin to that of a ballerina, terns hover before plunging into the watery depths for a fishy delight.

Be inspiring

SNOW BUNTING

Threading a delicate song among the snowy landscape,
this compact, finch-like bird is a symbol of hope, being
one of the first birds to return in the spring after a long
winter. Easily missed amid the thick snow of the Arctic
tundra thanks to its mostly pure white plumage, snow
buntings are passerine, meaning they can navigate the
rough terrain and run at speed, jumping should the need
arise. Just as well when you are a ground dweller that
tends to forage for food along the rocky shoreline.

Stay focused

TRUMPETER SWAN

Being the largest swan in the world is quite a feat for any waterfowl, especially when you consider that the trumpeter was once endangered thanks to the fashion for feathers in hats. That said, this swan rallied and increased its numbers and has now extended its range. Although impressively large, it carries itself with grace, courting an elevated, upright neck and an abundance of downy white feathers. Due to its immense size, this bird needs a lengthy 100-metre runway to get off the ground. Keeping its objective in mind, it gallops at speed along the surface of the waves until, with tenacity, it rises into the air.

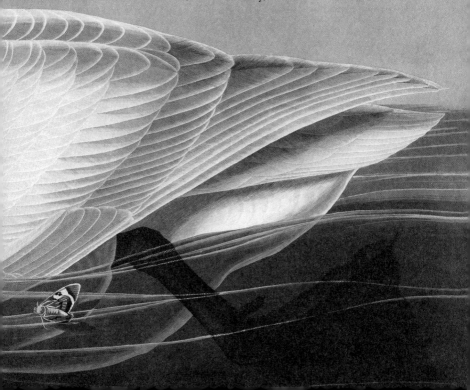

Give thanks for small pleasures

WOOD THRUSH

An operatic bird with a melodious song, which most agree
sums up the essence of nature, the jovial wood thrush is
at home in dense woodland, making their nests in the
shade to conceal and protect their young. This attractive,
medium-sized bird enjoys giving back, with flute-like arias
to serenade those who might cross their path. Its scientific
mantel means 'weasel-coloured woodland thrush' but it
is also known as the swamp angel, song thrush and wood
robin. Should you be lucky enough to encounter this
speckled marvel, take a moment to appreciate its gifts.

Keep your mind active

COMMON RAVEN

Sheathed in glossy darkness, the raven is a bird of mystery and a portent of death in many cultures. With a sharp mind and the cognitive skills to solve problems and express empathy with other members of its flock, this clever, charismatic bird uses its voice to mimic the cries of others, including humans. It's no wonder, therefore, that the raven was revered and seen as a spirit messenger. The Norse god Odin was often depicted with two ravens, one on each shoulder. It was said that every morning they would fly out into the world and bring back news and wisdom.

Celebrate your differences

ATLANTIC PUFFIN

If ever there was a comedian of the avian realm, then the title would go to the puffin. This stocky, short-winged parrot of the sea stands out from the crowd with its brightly coloured beak and clown-like appearance. That said, the puffin is perfectly adapted

to cope with the water, charging through the waves at speed, using its webbed feet as paddles to propel it forwards. It cares not about its peculiarities and excels by making the most of these unique differences. In spring and summer, it gathers with others of its kind in colonies along the coast of the North Atlantic.

Be bold in your endeavours

WILD TURKEY

According to renowned statesman and Founding Father, Benjamin Franklin, the wild turkey is blessed with immense courage and is a more fitting national emblem for America than the bald eagle. This grand, fine-feathered bird may look cumbersome, but it is a capable flier and able to reach up to 60 miles (97 kilometres) per hour in the air. Also gifted with supreme eyesight and a 270-degree field of vision, the turkey is surprisingly astute and able to see much further than other birds, which helps it avoid predators in the wild.

Identify your needs

COMMON REDPOLL

Peek beneath the willow thickets, in among the reed-like shrubs, and you might glimpse a scarlet-tipped finch with gentle brown streaks and a pinkish breast staring back at you. This beguiling beauty, known as the common redpoll, is commonly found nesting in the Arctic, and loves tall deciduous forests where it can flit about in safety. Able to cope with freezing temperatures thanks to its ability to eat up to 42 per cent of its body mass each day, the redpoll knows what it needs to survive, thrive and enjoy life.

Speak up when it matters

BLUE JAY

Like a shimmering sapphire, the blue jay brings a jewel-
like brightness to the dullest of days, and while the
colour of its plumage is certainly eye-catching, the
blue is merely a trick of the light caused by the barbed
surface of its feathers beneath the sun's scattered rays. A
loud and vibrant songbird with a reputation for being a
chatterbox, in truth the jay is quiet during nesting time.
But should a predator like a red-shouldered hawk appear,
it will alert other birds in the area by imitating its cries.

Strut your stuff

GREATER FLAMINGO

As the most widespread species of the flamingo family,
it's no surprise that the greater flamingo is a sociable sort
who enjoys expressing itself in the company of others.
Known as a flamboyance of flamingos when seen together,
this lofty bird with its elegant stance is also known for
colourful dance moves, which it perfects in order to win a
mate. With at least 136 manoeuvres used during courtship,
the greater flamingo is a stylish partner. This, coupled with
the flashy pink feathers, puts it firmly in the spotlight.

Make nature your haven

WHIPPOORWILL

This coppice-lover feels at home in the thick of the trees, and nests upon the ground between roots and leaves. Known for its plaintiff cry, the elusive whippoorwill is often seen as a ghostly creature that haunts the forest at night. While it is nocturnal, feeding mainly on insects at dusk, it is far from ominous. It gets its name from the male's unique wail, which comes in three separate notes: 'whip ... poor ... will'.

Be spontaneous

ANNA'S HUMMINGBIRD

It's no wonder this bird was named after the Duchess
of Rivoli, Anna Massena, when you consider its
regal appearance. The male is the most resplendent,
bearing iridescent emerald green back feathers and
a rosy red crown that it dons with aplomb. Flighty
and fast, with a wing beat of 40 to 50 beats per
second, this aerial wonder may be petite, but it has the
speediest diving flight of any bird and loves to whip
up a frenzy in the air. Synonymous with healing and
playfulness, it dares you to let your spontaneity soar.

Learn how to multitask

BARN SWALLOW

It may be pretty to look at with its blue outer plumage,
but the delicate barn swallow is a hive of industry.
It winters in South America and has surfaced as far
south as Argentina. This resourceful flier eats on the
wing, snatching insects mid-flight, no doubt to save
time and boost energy levels, and it's a keen recycler,
reusing old nests year after year. This tiny songbird
appreciates the importance of multitasking, and this
allows it to produce two broods of well-fed chicks,
one after the other. No wonder it's the national bird of
Estonia and Austria, and synonymous with good luck.

Find enjoyment in the little things

AMERICAN ROBIN

A cheerful bird with a distinctive sweet tooth, robins are
often seen enjoying fermented berries, which do make
them slightly tipsy! While it may bear the same name,
this species is unrelated to the European robin, coming
instead from the thrush family. Colonial settlers noted that
both birds sported a fiery chest and so gifted it the same
moniker. With its beautiful song and vibrant red underparts
that are often likened to embers, it was associated with
the element of fire, and thought to be the harbinger of
spring, being easy to spot at the turn of the season.

Let your actions reinvent you

WESTERN KINGBIRD

Formerly known as the Arkansas kingbird, this yellow-bellied beauty travels far and wide to snap up tasty insects, and was eventually given the 'western' title as a nod to its extensive travels over North America and as far south as Mexico. A voracious feeder who enjoys a variety of insects, the kingbird uses poles, wires and other humanmade structures as a perch to survey its aerial kingdom. Not a fan of other birds, the feisty kingbird will emit a loud buzzing warning call to put off interlopers.

Don't be afraid to make an impression

CAROLINA PARAKEET

Although declared extinct in 1939, this enigmatic bird certainly left an impression as a colourful character in every sense. Travelling in flocks of up to a thousand, Carolina parakeets made quite the cacophony and could be heard from miles away. That said, it was more sedate in the day, preferring to roost, bathe and rest in the trees. An expert climber, this joyful bird used its sturdy beak to grip and navigate the bark. In 2019 the bird's genome was sequenced as a potential candidate for de-extinction.

Share the love

MOURNING DOVE

With its slender body and muted hues, this graceful bird
has a gentle, soothing aura. Coupled with the calming
tone of its 'cooing', this makes it a pleasant addition
to any garden. Primarily a seed eater, it will stockpile
grains from the ground in its 'crop', an extended part of
its gullet, to digest later. Recognized around the world
as a symbol of peace and love, mourning doves, also
known as turtle doves, mate for life and can often be seen
snuggling up in their cherished twosome for comfort.

Be still and let your inner voice speak

MOUNTAIN QUAIL

For some spotters, the mythic mountain quail is elusive, conspicuous by its absence and notoriously hard to see in the wild. That's because this secretive bird tends to stick to the safety of dense bushland and when approached will remain under cover and completely motionless. Preferring to hang out in small numbers and never venturing too far, the mountain quail might appear shy at first, but it is simply content to keep its own counsel. As the name might suggest, this bird thrives in mountains and desertland.

Believe in yourself

AMERICAN KESTREL

Associated with sharp wit, patience and perseverance
thanks to its hunting prowess, this raptor proves that
you can be a fierce and fabulous contender whatever
your size. The Irish Celts called this diminutive bird
'pocaire gaoithe', meaning 'wind-frolicker', and while this
version is the smallest of its kind in North America,
it too is often referred to as a 'windhover' thanks to
its ability to hang in mid-air while sizing up its prey.
Once the location is determined with precision,
this little powerhouse will swoop in for the kill.

Hold your head high

RED-THROATED LOON

The smallest of all the loons, this sleek waterbird has a distinctive red throat during breeding season, and a smooth grey head. A keen diver, this loon takes to the water with the ease and grace of a prima ballerina, and coasts with its delicate bill tipped upwards. Perhaps this is to show off its famous russet patch when it can, or simply because it takes pride in its glide. Unlike other loons, it can take off from land and is also an adept flier.

Often seen in ponds and estuaries from late autumn through to spring, it frequents the northern hemisphere.

Spread happiness wherever you go

EASTERN BLUEBIRD

A flash of azure brightness across the sky, the bluebird
comes with blessings and is seen as a good omen in
folklore around the world. Its pretty cobalt plumage
may be a part of its charm, but there are other factors
at play. This bluebird is compact, with a strong centre
of gravity and a developed voicebox, which allows it
to sing the sweetest tunes. Being so perfectly balanced,
it belongs to a family of perching birds, singing and
flitting from tree to post throughout the day.

Lift others up

HARRIS'S HAWK

The Harris's hawk has many predators, including
coyotes, bobcats and great horned owls, but this
resilient bird has worked out a system of defence –
groups from the same flock will sound the alarm and
harass any eager opportunists. They also build their

nests high off the ground in the saguaro cactus for this reason. Protection is key, and these agile hawks practise a behaviour known as 'back standing', where they stand on top of each other and extend their wings to provide shade and shelter. This also means the top bird can warn the others of impending attack.

Engage with the world around you

GREY CATBIRD

'Curiosity killed the cat', so the saying goes, but birds are also blessed with an inquisitive nature and love to connect with their surroundings. While the grey catbird is generally shy and will zip into the nearest thicket if approached by a human, it can be summoned with a gentle 'pishing' sound. This little charmer can't resist a sneaky peak and likes to know what's going on in its environment. It's often seen amid the bushes, immersed in the foliage or hopping from tree to shrub. But don't expect to hear a tweet – this bird sounds like a cat and emits a bright mewing signature call.

Make the most of your assets

FORK-TAILED FLYCATCHER

The combination of a tiny black-capped head, diminutive body and an exceptionally long forked tail two or three times its body length might seem at odds with each other, but this pretty bird is a speed freak and one of the fastest in the world. Able to fly at speeds of up to 65 miles (105 kilometres) per hour, the fork-tailed flycatcher does exactly what it says on the tin, finding its balance in the air and using its enormous tail to steer, turn and snatch its prey. Coming from the tropics, it favours forests and grasslands, where it tends to perch in the highest trees.

Get organized

WHITE-BREASTED NUTHATCH

Should you see a delicate white-breasted bird scooting
along a tree trunk against the grain of the bark, it is most
likely a white-breasted nuthatch doing what it does
best – cracking open nuts and acorns by jamming them
into crevices until the shell splits open. This clever bird is
meticulously organized when it comes to foraging and
works in groups with other species like chickadees and
titmice to get the best results. It uses available resources,
like the security of its fellow avians and hardwearing
tree bark, to secure and enjoy a hearty meal.

Don't worry if you're not someone's cup of tea

BLACK-BILLED MAGPIE

No other bird divides opinion more than this monochrome mystery, and with its striking colourways and iridescent gleam it is a beauty to behold. There are those who fear its presence, seeing it as a bad omen and linked to witchcraft, a belief that was rife in the Middle Ages. While some, like the Manchu dynasty, who governed China from the seventeenth century, thought it fortuitous and adopted the bird as a symbol of imperial rule. Whatever your view, the magpie cares not, for it continues to thrive and is a common sight in gardens, farmland and grassland throughout the world.

Stake out your territory

ROCK PTARMIGAN

This hardy bird, not dissimilar to a hen, is found in the furthest northern reaches of the world from Alaska, Canada and Greenland to Scandinavia and Russia. A stocky individual belonging to the grouse family, it is known as the *'Raicho'* in Japan, meaning 'thunder bird'. Perhaps this is due to the powerful croaking noise the male emits during mating season, or the forceful flapping dance performed to protect its territory. A resilient bird with attitude to match its sturdy stature, it's predated by arctic foxes, golden eagles and snowy owls.

Anchor yourself

RED-BREASTED NUTHATCH

Compact and bijou, this tiny bird has robust, wiry claws
that allow it to get a firm grip by digging deep into the
roughest tree bark. Stabilizing itself in this way means the
nuthatch can show off its dexterity, hanging upside down
and climbing head first down the length of the trunk. This
also gives it the flexibility to collect the resin globules from
hardy coniferous trees that are used to line the entrance
of the nest hole. With a daring black and white stripe
above the eye, this little wonder has superhero style.

Go where your heart takes you

BOHEMIAN WAXWING

It's easy to see the origins of this bird's name when you consider its fine-feathered plumage. From the burnished red tips on its wings to the golden-flecked tailfeather ends, it looks as if it has been hand-dipped in wax to seal its beauty. The wandering ways of this aerial vagabond helps it attain the bohemian part of its mantel. Not one to shy away from change, it will travel great distances in search of its favourite rowan berries, and even conquer new vistas if that's what it takes to find sustenance.

Clarity comes with an open mind

SNOWY OWL

Often referred to as the arctic ghost because of its snowy white feathers, this bird swoops over the frozen tundra in search of sustenance. Unlike other owls, it hunts in the day and prefers the clarity of wide-open spaces rather than clusters of trees. Associated with vision and good fortune in many mythologies thanks to the purity of its feathers and its keen eyesight, the snowy owl navigates wintry landscapes with ease.

Seize opportunities

HERRING GULL

Boisterous and bossy, or so it might seem to the human
outsider, the herring gull frequents the North Atlantic
coastline throughout Europe, Scandinavia, and even
as far as Panama. With its bulky frame and grey and
white colouring, it's easy to spot and doesn't shy away
from attention. A notorious squabbler, it vies for fishy
treats, and has even been known to bait its own dinner.
According to onlookers at a Paris pond, one crafty
gull used morsels of bread to lure hungry goldfish
to the surface for an impromptu fast-food feast.

Be patient and keep going

COMMON SNIPE

This pale striped beauty knows you have to take your time and dig deep to find the gold, which in this case might be a tasty mollusc or crustacean. Probing the muddy straits with its oversized beak, the snipe is not easy to spot, blending into the marshy surroundings thanks to the intricate patterns of its coat. While it might be overlooked by some, this patient wader cares not, preferring to stay out of the limelight while it forages. Widespread throughout the world, including Europe, Asia, eastern Russia, the Indian subcontinent and also the Middle East and parts of Africa, the snipe thrives with quiet confidence.

Stay active

DOWNY WOODPECKER

This woodpecker is a petite powerhouse of movement and activity. Able to perform acrobatic manoeuvres while scaling the trees thanks to its diminutive stature, it pummels the tree bark up to ten times a second, and also creates a special drumming sound when trying to attract a mate. All this frenetic action could result in injury, but the downy woodpecker has a spongy shock pad between its skull and bill to protect the brain, and special protective feathers which surround the nostrils and prevent the inhalation of wood chips. No wonder it's a symbol of hard work and energy!

Know when to stand out or step back

HORNED GREBE

This striking bird is the bearer of horns formed by bright
yellow feathers, which it manipulates depending on its
mood. It dons a colourful plumage during the breeding
season, but swaps this for a more monochrome appearance
at other times, when it needs to fade into the landscape
for safety's sake, or to protect its young. Chicks often ride
on the backs of their parents, snuggling within the feathers
for safety. From this position, they can plunge under water
and experience the joy of a dive without the danger.

Find your unique style

CRESTED AUKLET

This fine-looking bird, which can be seen here on the bottom right of the picture, likes to wear its crest with feathered flair and is the social butterfly of the

bird world. The tufted plume, which hangs forwards
from the forecrown, is what sets it apart. The larger
the crest, the more likely the bird will secure a date
and a mate for life, although they do go solo at sea,
coming back together each year at the nesting site.

Work to your strengths

BROWN BOOBY

The booby gets its name from the Spanish word *'bobo'* meaning stupid, which seems unfair when you consider the success of this large sea bird. Breeding on islands and coasts throughout the Atlantic and Pacific oceans and favouring tropical climates, this charming bird is gregarious and will hunt for food by plunge-diving in flocks or solo, depending on the circumstance. Its aerial manoeuvres may be dexterous, but once it hits the ground the booby appears clumsy, hence it's somewhat shallow moniker. This seabird works to its strengths and uses strong winds to assist take-off and landing.

Centre yourself

SNOWY EGRET

Also known as the lesser egret, and little snowy, this
beautiful bird carries itself with poise and elegance.
While its pure white plumage makes it stand out from
the crowd, it was hunted for the beauty of its feathers
during the nineteenth century. Belonging to the heron
family, its slender neck creates an 'S' shape when flying.
This, coupled with its signature one-legged stance while
looking for fish, give it an almost ethereal quality. Being
able to thrive within the three elements of earth, air and
water, the snowy egret is a symbol of balance and focus.

Soothe your soul with silence

MANGROVE CUCKOO

As the name would suggest, this cuckoo inhabits the thick swarthy vegetation found in black and red swampy mangrove forests, ranging from Florida through to the Caribbean islands, Mexico and Central and South America. Seeking solace among the loftiest branches, it sits silent and still, waiting for prey to enter its domain. So quiet is this bird that it barely moves or vocalises when foraging, only tipping its head slightly should it spot something of interest. Slender and long-tailed in appearance, the mangrove cuckoo knows the restorative power of silence.

Let your inner beauty shine through

GLOSSY IBIS

The ibis is associated with Thoth, the ancient Egyptian god of writing and wisdom, and while this reveals the bird's astuteness, the glossy breed has even more to offer. On first appearance it can appear dull and leggy, but a closer inspection reveals a bloom of iridescent shades, from deep violet hues to glimmering, sun-kissed bronze. Being something of a nomadic wanderer, this wader tends to up sticks after breeding, dispersing further afield to expand its range.

Treat yourself!

NORTHERN PARULA

This long-distance migrant likes to spend its winters in the Caribbean, and who can blame it? A fan of tropical forests, it seeks the security of coffee, cacao and citrus plantations, and enjoys flitting among the forest canopy for fun. While this vibrant bird knows what it likes, it's fairly solitary during the breeding season. That said, you'll be able to hear its joyful tune above your head – this wood warbler's forte is trilling loudly as it dances between the branches, no doubt expressing it's delight at the sheer exuberance of life.

Be your own cheerleader

KING EIDER

While these spectacular ducks favour the Arctic tundra
for breeding, they can generally be found in North
America, Europe and Asia. With their striking good
looks, it's no wonder their species name *spectabilis*
means 'showy' and 'remarkable'. The king eider wears
its crown with attitude and a matching forehead bulge
thanks to a large plate positioned above the bill. While
this might suggest they're big-headed, it simply adds to
their forthright character. Highly expressive, the king
eider has a vast range of vocal sounds, from grunting,
growling and quacking to dove-like coos when mating.

Play to your strengths

OSPREY

When an osprey sets its sight upon its prey, there's no escape. This expert angler uses its feet to catch fish just beneath the water, rotating its toes backwards to ensure a tight grip on its slippery supper. This, along with super sharp talons and tiny spiny points on the inner surface of each foot, helps to secure its catch. Perhaps this is why it is often called a 'fish hawk'. With a wide distribution throughout the world, you can usually see it along sea coasts, wetlands and marshes. Its lofty nest, usually built on treetops or telephone poles, is a massive structure from which it surveys its watery kingdom.

Remember to rest and recharge

DOUBLE-CRESTED CORMORANT

This is the low rider of water birds, preferring to keep most of its body submerged beneath the surface of the water, though it lets its long neck and head peep above as it glides. The cormorant seeks out large areas of water, like lagoons and lakes that are abundant with fish, to take up residence and spends almost half of its time fishing and feeding so that it can rest and digest for the other half of the day. These birds like to recharge by stretching out their wings beneath the sun so that their feathers can dry thoroughly.

There is a purpose to everything

BLACK VULTURE

The hardiest of birds, built with purpose and precision, the black vulture is a masterpiece in the making and synonymous with protection. While some may be repulsed by its dark skulking frame and bald head, there is a wonderfully morbid reason for its unusual appearance – the exposed skin is much easier to clean after feeding from a carcass. Vultures cleanse the environment by gorging on rotting meat, after which their powerful stomach acids eradicate bacteria, leaving fungal-free faeces. With a giant 5-foot wingspan, this dark brooding shadow is the guardian of the animal kingdom.

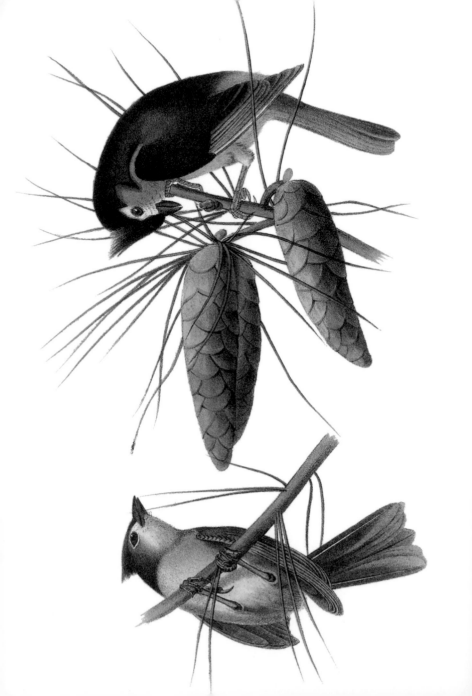

Make time for family

TUFTED TITMOUSE

When other birds use their alarm call it tends to draw their predators to them, but the clever titmouse has perfected the ability to throw its voice, sending hungry assailants off into the distance. A charming little bird with large penetrating eyes, it does its bit for the environment too by spreading tree seed and keeping problem insects in check. At least one of the titmouse's young will stay with its parents to help out with the next brood of chicks, and sometimes errant juveniles will join a family grouping for this purpose.

Make your home your happy place

CAROLINA WREN

Like most wrens, this little beauty has a distinctive song and is a frequent visitor to gardens and bird feeders. Coming from the troglodyte family, meaning 'cave dweller', it prefers its cavities to be nestled within tree bark. Even so, this makes a snug substitute and a safe place for this bird to set up home, which it does with ease, usually laying between three and seven eggs. During incubation the male feeds the female while serenading her.

Pay attention to your surroundings

HORNED LARK

It may have a brown body for the most part, but take a closer look and you'll see a striking facial mask with a black and yellow pattern, along with the distinctive black horns which the male dons in summer. This curious little bird prefers to walk along the vast desert tundra sooner than hop like its feathered friends. In taking its time, it can carefully scour the earth for those hard-to-find insects. Also found in fields, meadows and farmland, the horned lark is a delightful songbird that pays attention to its environment in order to blend in.

Tap into your wild side

PAINTED BUNTING

If you peer among a tangle of weeds, or forage in the scrub,
you might be lucky enough to see a rainbow of colours
streaking beneath the undergrowth. The painted bunting
may be a masterpiece when it comes to its pretty plumage,
but it feels most at home in the wild places. Flying within
its flock or hiding from predators, it seems that this striking
bird enjoys being immersed in nature, feral and free. Native
to North America, it migrates when the colder weather
comes, travelling as far as Mexico, the Caribbean and Cuba.

Listen mindfully

GREAT GREY OWL

Found in dense coniferous forests, this large mottled
grey owl is one of the tallest in the world. A circular
facial disc gives it a distinctive and somewhat spectral
appearance, but there is a reason for this. The feathers,
which are positioned in a spherical dial, span outwards
directing all sound to the ears. This accentuates the owl's
already keen hearing, allowing it to listen and create a
sound map of its prey. With a soft lilting hoot, this gentle
giant casts a shadow on the landscape and reminds us
that listening is more important than making noise.

Look at things from a different perspective

WHITE-WINGED CROSSBILL

A colourful character with a vivid reddish-pink plumage and lots of attitude, the white-winged crossbill, also known as the two-barred crossbill in Europe, favours spruce, tamarack and fir trees. Feasting upon conifer seeds daily is what it does best, along with aerial acrobatics, which includes hanging upside down, parrot-style, from the tips of trees. From this unique position it gets a clearer view of the forest beneath and any interlopers in its territory. A change in perspective helps it protect its brood and food, and spot fallen pinecones on which to snack.

Nurture yourself and others

NORTHERN CARDINAL

Whether it's a bit of self-care, or being looked after by a loved one, everyone needs a dose of TLC from time to time. With its blood red plumage, the male cardinal adds a splash of colour wherever it goes. The female may be a little muted in her pale brown, but there's a warm red glow to her feathers, and what she lacks in brightness she makes up for in melody. Unlike other female songbirds, this beauty sings her heart out while on the nest, usually to indicate that she needs food, which the male delivers in abundance. Sometimes her song is as an alarm call, and sometimes it's simply because she's happy nurturing and being nurtured by her mate.

Don't miss what's right in front of you

FOX SPARROW

These sturdy little birds come in a range of shades from rust red to slate grey, and even a deep brown 'sooty' variety, but while the hues depend on their habitat (with the reddest favouring boreal forests) they have one thing in common – they love to forage. Usually spotted scratching around in the scrub using both legs to kick away dead leaves, this confident bird can spot a hidden morsel beneath the detritus of the forest floor. Slightly bigger than its European counterpart, it bears mottled markings and streaks and a medium-length tail.

Strive to reach new heights

CALIFORNIA CONDOR

The California condor may be a scavenger, but it does it in style, gliding with epic grace through the North American skyline. Commonly seen frequenting rocky outcrops and forests in the states of California, Arizona, Utah and the Mexican state of Baja California, it has a gigantic wingspan of 10 feet. No wonder it is sometimes mistaken for an aircraft. While you might assume its breathtaking size would render it clumsy, its upturned wing-feather tips reduce the drag and create a smooth, seamless flight. Just what you'd expect from a bird that survived extinction during the Ice Age.

Maintain an air of mystery

SCARLET TANAGER

There's nothing like a little evasiveness to pique
interest. Like any rare jewel, the scarlet tanager is hard
to find even for the most experienced eye, which is
surprising when you consider its bright ruby hue. This
secretive bird likes to hang out in the forest canopy
and favours the sleek loftiness of hemlocks and pines,
where it moves sedately so as not to attract attention.

Tap into your intuition

AMERICAN CROW

Closely related to the collard crows of China and the
carrion crow of Europe, this glossy-winged corvid still
has many distinguishing features. It's coal black plumage
and high-pitched caw are an instant giveaway, along
with its sharp, intelligent eyes that help it to scavenge
and hunt its prey. No wonder this intuitive bird is often
called the trickster. A companion to the Mayan god of
thunder and lightning, and a cohort of the Greek god
of the sun, Apollo, the crow is seen as a favourable omen
in Japan, where it is considered a divine messenger.

Index

American
crow
p.124

American
goldfinch
p.14

American
kestrel
p.53

American
robin
p.42

Anna's
hummingbird
p.39

Arctic tern
p.17

Atlantic puffin
p.26

Barn swallow
p.40

Belted
kingfisher
p.9

Black-billed
magpie
p.67

Black vulture
p.103

Blue jay
p.32

Bohemian
waxwing
p.73

Brown booby
p.87

California
condor
p.121

Carolina
parakeet
p.47

Carolina wren
p.106

Common
raven
p.25

Common
redpoll
p.31

Common
snipe
p.79

| Crested auklet p.84 | Double-crested cormorant p.100 | Downy woodpecker p.80 | Eastern bluebird p.57 | Fork-tailed flycatcher p.63 |

| Fox sparrow p.118 | Glossy ibis p.92 | Greater flamingo p.35 | Great grey owl p.112 | Grey catbird p.60 |

| Harris's hawk p.58 | Herring gull p.76 | Horned grebe p.82 | Horned lark p.108 | King eider p.97 |

| Mangrove cuckoo p.91 | Manx sheerwater p.10 | Mountain quail p.50 | Mourning dove p.48 | Northern cardinal p.117 |

Northern
parula
p.94

Osprey
p.98

Painted
bunting
p.111

Prothonotary
warbler
p.13

Red-breasted
nuthatch
p.70

Red-throated
loon
p.54

Rock
ptarmigan
p.68

Scarlet tanager
p.123

Snow bunting
p.18

Snowy egret
p.88

Snowy owl
p.74

Trumpeter
swan
p.20

Tufted
titmouse
p.105

Western
kingbird
p.44

Whippoorwill
p.36

White-breasted
nuthatch
p.64

White-winged
crossbill
p.114

Wild turkey
p.28

Wood thrush
p.22